Our Past, Our Way!

by
LAURENE RAGSDALE

Published By Tierra Destiny Reid and TDR Brands Publishing

TITLE:
Our Past, Our Way!

AUTHOR:
Laurene Ragsdale

PUBLISHED BY:
Tierra Destiny Reid and TDR Brands Publishing

EDITOR:
Cary Steiner

ISBN:
978-1-947574-84-7

AUTHOR:
Laurene Ragsdale

PRINTED IN THE UNITED STATES OF AMERICA

Copyright © 2024 **Laurene Ragsdale**

All rights reserved. This book is copyright material and must not be copied, reproduced, transferred, distributed, leased, licensed or used in any way except as specifcally permitted in writing by the author, as allowed under the terms and conditions under which it was purchased or as strictly permitted by applicable copyright law. Respective authors own all copyrights not held by the publisher. In no way is it legal to reproduce, duplicate, or transmit any part of this document in either electronic means or printed format.

Any unauthorised distribution or use of this text may be a direct infringement of the Author's rights, and those responsible may be liable in law accordingly.

DEDICATION

This is a heartfelt tribute honoring my ancestors for enduring the journey from Africa through Europe to the U.S., celebrating their strength and wisdom. It honors my grandparents: Emmitt and Laura Arnwine and their children, especially my aunts for their love, guidance, discipline and resilience. Their stories reflect perseverance through hardships like the Great Depression, the Jim Crow era and the Civil Rights Movement, inspiring our family as most lived well into their 80s and 90s.

Daughters gone but not forgotten:
Sarah A. Clay
Farilla A. McCowan
Emmittee A. Ragsdale
Elmar A. Tilley
Ruth A. Whitaker
Freddye A. Cairo

Daughter still with us:
Effie A. Clark

CONTENTS

Part One: *The Midwife's Book*

9

Part Two: *Keepers*

27

Part Three: *Intentional Journaling Prompts*

39

Part Four: *Quotes*

53

Part Five: *Additional Resources*

85

Part Six: *Meet the Author*

91

Part One:
The Midwife's Book

"Do you folks have Miss Laura's original book?"

"What book?"

"The book that she wrote all of the births in."

Nobody knew where the book was.

Miss Laura was my grandmother, Laura Lee Freeman Arnwine (Freeman was her maiden name). I knew I was named after her. But as a child, I knew nothing about her work life.

She had passed in 1959, and I wasn't born until later, so she was gone when I got here. No one told me what she had done, and I hadn't asked.

I grew up living on a Farm-To-Market road in the Mount Haven Community, a Piney Woods region of East Texas, and the first time I heard that my grandmother had been a midwife was from a neighbor who lived about a quarter-mile down the road. My mom didn't let me visit people very often, but this one day (which had to have been a

Sunday), I got to visit my friends at their grandmother's home, the home of J. C. Jr. and Parthenia Jones. In the South, we tend to cut things off and stretch words out, so we always pronounced it Potheenie, but it was really Mrs. Parthenia.

I don't recall how it came about, but Miss Parthenia said, "Miss Laura birthed all my babies."

I looked up at her and asked, "Huh? She birthed all your babies?"

"Yeah," she said, "Miss Laura brought all my babies into the world."

Miss Parthenia had five children: Bobbie Jean, Billy Ray, JoAnne, J. C. Jr., and Linda Gail—and I may not have the order correct. You had to pass by Mr. Edgar and Bobbie Miles' house before you got to her mother's (Mrs. Parthenia's). Billy Ray, Linda Gail and J. C. Jr. are still living.

I took note when Mrs. Parthenia said that my grandmother

had birthed all her babies. I was a very inquisitive kid, but I didn't know what to do with that. I was young, so I went home and asked more questions.

Home for me was the house that my mother and all her six sisters grew up in. We called it the family home; we also call it the "Rock House."

Aunt Faye had her hair salon at the back of the house and we all lived in the family house together, so I always had two mothers at home at all times.

At home that day were my mom, my Aunt Sarah, the oldest, and my Aunt Faye, the hairdresser and next oldest sister. And when I asked, they all said, "Oh, yes, she went to a lot of people's houses to deliver their babies. She was a midwife!"

I don't know what else came up in that conversation, but I was impressed.

A lot of people used to come by on the weekends; cousins, neighbors, and friends or former classmates of

my mother and aunts. They would come by to visit or to ask about the other sisters, because this was the family home and everyone knew one of the sisters would be home at some point to visit with the sisters who still lived at the rock house. One day, somebody asked about my grandmother's 'book.'

I was eavesdropping. As I said, I was an inquisitive little girl.

"Do you folks have Miss Laura's original book?"

"What book?"

"The book that she put all of the births in."

Everybody got quiet. I thought then that nobody knew where the book was. I later figured that if anybody did know where the book was, they weren't saying. That's my take on the situation now.

I wondered about that book. I knew people wanted it, but neither of the sisters ever confessed to knowing

where it was.

I pictured a big, hardbound black book, like a journal or a family bible. It had to be somewhere.

Four or five decades passed, and eventually, the only sisters left were my Aunt Elmar and Aunt Effie, and we all moved to Waxahachie to live together.

At some point after the move, I was going through a lot of Rubbermaid storage bins full of stuff, things we had just moved and put over to the side back in 2018-2019 because it was just time to de-clutter the Rock House.

So I said, let's go through these boxes and bins while we have some free time together.

I found one of those messenger bags in one of the bins, like the Western Union telegram people used to carry back in the day. It was old and worn out, and the strap was broken. It smelled something awful — old and musty or moldy — so I put on gloves and a mask before I reached into it. When I opened the bag, it smelled worse.

Inside the bag, Aunt Elmar said what I found was smelling salts, and a tube what looked like a glass syringe that would fit on a needle to give someone an injection. There were other items, all quite old.

I found a letter. The paper was old, like onion skin paper, but not quite as thin. It had a rubber stamp at the top that said:

H.D. Patton, M.D.
901 S Fulton St. Palestine, Texas

Under that was a handwritten note:

July 22nd, 1950

To Whom It May Concern:

This certifies that Mrs. Laura L. Arnwine has had the practical experience and training which qualifies her to be a midwife and do deliveries of babies.
Respectfully,
H.D. Patton, M.D.

The signature was all jumbled together, the way doctors and lawyers write, but the handwriting itself was pretty legible.

And lo and behold, with the letter, I found the book. I don't know if my heart beat faster, but I knew I was excited. There I was, at the dining room table of the house in Waxahachie, and I said out loud, "Oh my God, this is it. This is the book!"

My two aunts looked at me. "What book? What are you talking about?"

"This is the book!" I was elated.

It was not a big, hardbound black journal but an old-fashioned Bluebird composition notebook.

The book is about 5"x7" with the word Bluebird across the top and a painting of two bluebirds on a tree branch. Underneath, it says "Composition Book," and at the very bottom, there's a box to write your name, school, and grade.

Inside the book is written, "Born to Mr. & Mrs. Mitchell McEwen, a boy," and the year, 1953. But on the next page, it says, "Borned to Mr. and Mrs. Travis Black, a boy," with the month and date, and the year is 1928. The child's name isn't listed, but I believe it's Dave Black, a cousin of ours who lived at the end of the road, almost to the railroad tracks, in the community we call Mount Haven, where I grew up.

The next one is listed in a similar way, but it's one of her own children. "Borned to Mr. and Mrs. E. Arnwine. A girl, August 19th, 1930, and it says, "Ruth Jean Arnwine."

So what I wonder still, did she deliver her own child? There is only one of her other children in the book, and that was the baby girl – Freddye. Aunt Effie, the only currently living daughter, who is now 92 years young, is not listed.

It's a mystery.

My grandmother's household consisted of a husband and seven daughters, and one son. She worked multiple

jobs, prepared and cooked the meals. She decided who would do the chores around the house and delegated accordingly. Then there was the gardening and delivering babies. To keep up with all of this and get little or no sleep was amazing of her now that I think about it. Life was so much harder back then but she persevered. I think my grandmother was just too busy with life to keep up with everything and the paperwork too. I asked Aunt Elmar, the 97-year-old, before she passed, "Who helped your mother when she was having her babies?"

"You know," she answered, "I don't know!"

Then she told me a story about when Aunt Ruth was born in 1930. Aunt Elmar, born in 1926, was in another room when her mother called her in one day and said, "Come on and look at the baby." Aunt Elmar said, "What baby?" Aunt Elmar goes in and looks at the baby. Her mother said, "What do you think?" Aunt Elmar said, "I didn't think nothing, and I just walked on out because it looked like a little old red rat!"

I laughed so hard I almost fell out of my chair. I knew

Aunt Ruth (who was the baby she was referring to) had the fairest skin color of all of her sisters, so this made so much sense that she looked like a little red rat at birth!

Aunt Elmar was the youngest child until Aunt Ruth was born, so you have to wonder: was this the beginning of the sibling rivalry? Think about that. Aunt Elmar always talked about how close she was to her mother, as if she was the only one close to their mom. I've seen the sibling rivalry between Aunt Elmar and Aunt Ruth my whole life, and this little story tells me that it has gone on since birth!

The next child listed in the book was a boy born to R.L. Green in April of the following year, 1931. After that, Mr. and Mrs. G.P. Gray had a boy in 1931, then Mr. and Mrs. Thurlan or Thurlow (some of them are hard to read) Silmon.

Two girls followed, one in 1931, then two children in '34, and the second one born in 1934 was "Borned to Mr. and Mrs. E. Arnwine, a girl, November 5, 1934." That was my Aunt Freddye, the baby girl.

My grandmother had four older daughters and a son before these two girls were born. Aunt Effie, born in 1932, isn't listed. My grandmother delivered a child into the world in 1931, and then the book jumps to 1933. So, I'm thinking that she probably didn't have time to do much midwifery from '31 to '33, especially with this many children and all her household duties, as well as her job.

It looks like she's listed all the names of the parents in the book. She numbered them all the way up to 124, about 20 or so births per page.

Many of these babies are still living, which is why I feel so protective of this book. These are birth records. Most of them are from the Mount Haven community, although when I was a child, I heard the family talk about it; they would say, "Oh, yes, she would travel all over the county!"

I was little then, and what did I know? I didn't even know what a county was, but it sounded like she journeyed far and wide!

"She would get up and go all hours of the night," they said. "Sometimes, the expectant mother's family would have to send someone other than a family member to pick up my grandmother and get her to the family's home. She would have to leave, even if she had worked that day and knew she would have to work the next day. She had to go deliver those babies!"

In the book, she had two of her children and two of her grandchildren. My mother gave birth to my brother Paul in 1945 and my brother Godfrey in 1947. I was the first of my mother's children who was not brought into the world by my grandmother, "the midwife."

I wonder, to this day, if my twin sister would have survived had my grandmother still been alive. I also wonder how afraid my mother must have been since she was used to having her mother's help delivering her children.

The book goes all the way up to November 16th, 1954. The last baby in the book was born to Mr. and Mrs. Woodrow Wilson Whitaker, a girl.

Over the years, we would talk about the book and all that was in it, and Aunt Elmar told me, "I used to help Mama write in that book." I know Aunt Elmar's handwriting, and I recognize that she wrote a lot of the names from 1952 through the last one in 1954.

Going through the book today, I see other familiar handwriting. I recognize my mother's handwriting from 1949, but I can't be absolutely sure it's hers.

All my mother's older sisters talked about how they used to help her with writing in the book.

The book, which I had imagined as a remarkable journal, is humble. The pages are old and tanned by age, almost as tan as a cardboard box. It wasn't well preserved, but I look after it now.

One day, I got a call from Miss Parthenia's granddaughter, Toni. We got to talking, and she told me about my Aunt Sarah, who was a teacher at the Mt. Haven Elementary School. All the kids in the community went to that Rosenwald-built school for Black children; you could see

the school from the dining room window of the Rock House, or if you stepped outside on the porch, or just stood in the yard. It was about a short city block away. Toni also told me a story about my grandmother. She said that when J. C. Jr., who they called Junior, was born, he didn't come out breathing, and my grandmother saved him.

This was news to me. "What do you mean," I asked. She told me the story so vividly, as though she'd been there. I didn't even think to ask if she'd been there. She said, "Well, Junior wasn't breathing, so to bring him back, she put him in a box inside the wood stove."

Back in the 1950s, people still had wood stoves in their houses. Wood stoves stayed hot for a long time and stayed warm even longer. I thought it was a drastic measure, but it probably wasn't, depending on the time of day he was born, and the book doesn't list the time of J. C. Jr.'s birth. Either way, it was my grandmother's version of the incubator, and was a smart move because J. C. Jr. survived.

So, between 1928 and 1954, my grandmother brought 124 children into this world that are documented. I've heard of other midwives who have documented 600 babies. Some birth books have been lost over time.

The book has Our Past; my family's past and the history of Black women in East Texas, in the South, in America. The story is told Our Way, in births recorded with humility and pride.

I was told it was hard to get a birth certificate done back in the day if you were Black. For instance, you had to prove you were born to get your retirement money, that became an issue.

It became an issue for my Aunt Freddye. They knew she was born on November 5th, 1934, but the documentation was in the book, and nobody knew where it was!
We tore the house up, trying to find that book. I do not know where the book was in the beginning. I do know it had been packed in a storage container when we moved to Waxahachie, Texas.

It was there all along. Could we have found it earlier if we had looked harder? Probably, but it was found in its time.

Part Two:
Keepers

My grandmother, my grandfather, my mother, and her sisters lived through the Great Depression, and saving things was important. I don't know if they kept things besides the book for historical purposes or not, but there were other compelling items in that same collection of papers.

I found a copy of *The Dallas Semi-Weekly Farm News*, dated Friday, May 25th, 1934. It's just a tattered newspaper with some interesting artwork behind the banner, and it's labeled as follows:

Ragsdale, B.B.
Route 4
Jacksonville, Texas

Apparently, Mr. Ragsdale, our Superintendent of the Mount Haven CME Church and a neighbor, subscribed to the Dallas Semi-Weekly Farm News.

Why did my grandmother keep this paper? Probably for the article headlined, "**...Barrow and Bonnie Parker Shot To Death In Lousiana...**" It's pretty obvious it was

Bonnie & Clyde! Inside, I can read "Clyde Barrow and Bonnie Parker... Longview, Texas, May 24th... Killers... Sanguinary trail was terminated in a blast of gunfire and death in a small rural Louisiana town Wednesday... frequently moved in and out of Gregg County, but so far as is known, their sorties into the sector were made as social calls on relatives and were bloodless."

So, I guess technically, my grandmother was a historian with that article and the book. But this newspaper article was just in a bag, a plain plastic bag that I remember was used for canning peas, tied with an old wire bread wrapper, long before Ziplocs were invented.

They kept a lot of stuff. There are a lot of letters. My Aunt Ruth, the first daughter listed in the book, kept all the letters her husband had written her before they got married, letters from 1955 and 1958.

So my relatives were sentimental if nothing else.
As we move, relocate, and de-clutter, I think it's essential that we stay mindful of the value of our keepsakes over

time. The records and items passed on to us need to be considered. What to keep? What are treasures? What should we preserve for the generations to come?

Don't throw the stuff out just because it's old. Look through it. Even though figuring out where to store stuff is a big deal for all of us, contemplate and appreciate why these things were saved and consider who might be interested in them in the future.

I found a trunk full of stuff; it must have been a hope chest for my mom. Back then, a woman kept a hope chest, a trunk or a box to store things for when they would get married.

In this trunk, I found a cooking pot, lingerie. I found cute little outfits, letters, wonderful things. Are they useful? Not at all. Are they keepers? Absolutely.

There are so many things boxed up. There are even giant old Bibles. And mind you, this stuff *smells*. It's been sitting for decades. My grandmother died in 1959, and this is 2024. That's 65 years unopened or opened

once and stacked on something else with something else stacked on it.

We went through my grandmother's trunk before Aunt Elmar's eyesight began to get worse. She could still see pretty well, even in 2011 and 2012. There were so many pictures, and I said, "Hey, we're going to write the names on the backs of these pictures."

So, we sat in the front with all four sisters: Aunt Elmar, Aunt Ruth, Aunt Effie and Aunt Freddye, and we wrote on each picture. I would ask Aunt Elmar, "Who is this? And who is this? And this?" I wrote the names on the back of each photo. I remember my brother Paul, who had been State Representative in Dallas in the 70s and early-to-mid-80s, was notorious for saying, "Date it! Write on it, who it is, because nobody will know who this is in fifty years." He was right. I even wrote 'unknown' on the back of pictures when Aunt Elmar did not know who the person or people were.

If you can save photos and have somewhere safe to store them, hang on to them because they are history. Your

past, certainly, but also our past, history told in the way only your family could tell it.

I went to a symposium a few months ago. The Department of Transportation did a presentation; they were trying to find elements of a community where they were about to construct a road. We know because history has shown that roads are built through our neighborhoods, highways are put through our neighborhoods, water is used to cover up our communities. We need to hang on to our history.

My grandmother was born in 1895. It was just after the reconstruction era, and slavery was still a clear, recent memory. By the 1920s, Blacks were building their own towns and communities, and my community of Mount Haven had already been created and was growing. Mount Haven was a community near the town of Jacksonville, Texas. The citizens had their own businesses and farms. People opened hair salons, mechanic garages, and taxicab companies in the town of Jacksonville. In our neighborhood, we had Nadine's store. We couldn't buy a lot of stuff there, but what I remember most as a

child was that she had cookies in plastic bins. You could take the top off and find what we called jack cookies, or oatmeal cookies, those were the best store-bought cookies.

People older than I remember even more about our Black communities, and we need to teach the next generation what they know and had to endure.

It was only sixty years after slavery, my grandmother had to help Black women deliver babies because there was no way a Black woman could go to a hospital to have a baby. I was the first of my mother's children to be born in a hospital.

That says a lot.

We haven't had much change.

And from the statistics I see, Black women are losing children in childbirth and dying in childbirth because there's no care or not enough people who care. I am being as polite as I can here.

The daughter of one of my friends was expecting. She'd had a baby before, and she went to a well-known hospital in Dallas. She kept telling the nurse to check her because she'd had an epidural and couldn't feel anything.
And the nurse said, "Oh no, honey, you don't have to worry. You're not due for hours now." My friend's daughter kept saying, "You should check. You should check."

Finally, the doctor came in to check. The baby had come out, was head down, and had turned blue. That baby survived for four years but was connected to machines for her entire life.

I told that story to my cousin's daughter, who was pregnant. My cousin got a little upset with me for telling her daughter a negative story while she was expecting, but ultimately this ended up helping her daughter to know the signs when the male nurse who 'helped' her during her second child's birth was flat-out rude and unhelpful.
Black women are, to this day, having a hard time during pregnancy and childbirth.

It's scary to know that there are still the same issues today that my mother and others had sixty to 100 years ago.

And I hope that women continue to be trained as midwives and doulas so they can assist and be there for the mothers of the next generation and then teach the next generation to do what they're doing. We must always have those who have the knowledge because women can't always get to the hospital. And the hospital isn't always the best place.

When my mother went to the hospital to give birth to me, they put her in the corridor. Someone from the Historical Commission in East Texas told me that putting Black women in labor in the hallway was standard procedure! Midwives and doulas need to teach the next generation. Find someone to be your protégé, your next-in-charge. Someday, something may happen to you, and we can't afford to lose your skills because you didn't pass on what you know.

It's still essential to have more than one skill set to

survive. My grandmother was a midwife, but she also worked at the meat locker, where people brought their cows and hogs to be slaughtered or butchered. And the front of the store was a butcher shop.

People learned in the Great Depression that you needed to have food and water, and they saved everything. I believe that's why I found so many artifacts, because my family members didn't throw very many things away. Learn about your ancestors. Ask questions. There's so much history that people don't talk about. My uncle Horace was a Montford Point Marine. We didn't know what that was until after he died. I had to Google it. They were the first Black U.S. Marines in World War II. If you look it up, here's what you'll find:

> *The Montford Point Marine Association is a nonprofit military veterans' organization, founded to memorialize the legacy of the first African Americans to serve in the United States Marine Corps. The first African American U.S. Marines were trained at Camp Montford Point, in Jacksonville, North Carolina, from 1941 to 1949.*

Uncle Horace was a Montford Point Marine. We did not know what that was until we were invited to a ceremony where that set of Marines was being honored by President Obama's team. His name was called at that ceremony. I have the medallion that was given during the ceremony. I was blessed to attend in his honor on behalf of the Arnwine side of the family – he was married to my Aunt Ruth.

The men who went into the military don't talk about it. My uncle Chauncey, Aunt Elmar's husband, was in the Army during World War II. He never talked about it. He went to church every Sunday. He taught Sunday School. He taught math in the public school system. But he never talked much about the war.

His wife, Aunt Elmar kept everything, too. I recently found all her records from college and every certificate she ever received from working as a teacher. I also found a grief journal. I had encouraged her to take a grief class because she and her husband Chauncey Tilley had been married for almost fifty years - to lose someone you have been with that long is very traumatic.

Your family members have been through trials, peaks, and valleys, and when you find these things or ask them questions, you give them the voice to tell their story.

To know that your family members couldn't walk down the same side of the street as a white woman, or they had to get off the sidewalk and walk in the road. That's their history.

It's eye-opening to find what I've been finding, to hear and remember the stories I've been told.

Everyone can be a keeper of history, and I encourage you to keep your family's past alive, because it's not just your past. It's our past, our way.

Part Three:
Intentional Journaling Prompts

Tell me about your childhood, what was life like growing up in your hometown or on the farm, in your community?

_____
_____
_____
_____

Are there any fond memories you have of you with your siblings?

_____
_____
_____
_____

Did you live in the City or in the country/ small community outside the city limits/ freedom colony, etc?

_____
_____
_____
_____

Was there a name everyone in that area knows for the area you grew up in?

_____
_____
_____
_____

What did your Mom and Dad do for a living?

_____
_____
_____
_____

Did your parents/grandparents own a business? Did they have a second job? If so, what did they do? Did they bake cakes, work on cars, launder clothes or sheets, etc. to make extra money? If so were they known for being the best baker or mechanic, launderer, etc? Are there any stories about them you have heard or a neighbor remembers? Best Apple pie, sweet potato pie, peach cobbler, best fried fish, etc.?

_____
_____
_____
_____

Were your grandparents/great grandparents enslaved?
_____
_____
_____
_____

What did your grandparents on your Mom's side do for a living?
_____
_____
_____
_____
_____

What did your parents on your dad's side do for a living?
_____
_____
_____
_____

Was there a special recipe that was handed down to you or your parents, grandparents?
_____
_____
_____
_____

Was there a piece of furniture/jewelry/etc. that you or your loved ones owned that has been passed down? A wedding ring, necklace, pocket watch, earrings, cuff links, etc.?

_____
_____
_____
_____

Are there any journals/diaries/letters that you or your family members still have? How are they being stored or digitized?

_____
_____
_____
_____

Was there something your mother/father/grandparents cooked or grilled that was especially memorable? Good or bad?

_____
_____
_____
_____

Was there a meal that you had to eat everyday because of you or your family's economic status?
Example my mother and her sisters ate a baked sweet potato everyday while in elementary school?

_____
_____
_____
_____

Were any family members in the military? If so, what branch? What was their rank? Were they sent to war? If so which war? How long did they serve in the military?

_____
_____
_____
_____

Was he/she honorably discharged?

_____
_____
_____
_____

If participated in a war, do they have any stories about that time?

_____
_____
_____
_____

Did they receive any awards? Purple Heart, certificates, etc.? Who trained them? For example, Madame C. J. Walker trained my Aunt the hairdresser?

_____
_____
_____
_____
_____

Are there any pictures of their work or finished product/s? Did people come from other nearby towns/cities to get that person's products/hair done?

_____
_____
_____
_____

What High Schools, Colleges, Universities did they attend? Did they graduate? Was it a HBCU, Ivy League, Junior College, Barber or Beauty College?

_____
_____
_____
_____
_____

Did they have a license? Master Plumber, Cosmetology, Barber's license?

_____
_____
_____
_____

If not a license were they handymen, midwives, carpenters, cooks, shoeshine men, chauffeurs, bus drivers, teachers?

_____
_____
_____
_____

Did they own their own business?

_____
_____
_____
_____

Did your relatives sew, crotchet, knit, or embroider, etc. Do you have anything the sewed, knitted, crocheted or embroidered?

_____
_____
_____
_____

Are there any people still living who they worked for? Ex: Barber or hairdresser who did their hair? Carpenter or Mason who built the house you or family members lived in?

_____
_____
_____
_____

If a farmer or sharecropper, where was the land that was farmed? Do they still own the land? Do you have the deeds, or any copies of paperwork about the land?

_____
_____
_____
_____

If a midwife, are there any children still living?

_____
_____
_____
_____

Is there a book of births or some type of record of the births? What years did the midwife assist with birthing?

_____
_____
_____
_____

Do the children have any stories about their birth? Or does anyone else remember a story about their sister or brother's birth?

_____
_____
_____
_____

Any embarrassing or funny stories you remember being told about yourself or your siblings? For example; was there a time when you/your parents caught you or someone else doing something they should not have been doing?

_____
_____
_____
_____

Was there any punishment from that experience or consequences for their actions?

_____
_____
_____
_____

Do you have any photos of your ancestors? How are they stored? Have they been digitized?
_____
_____
_____
_____

Did your parents or grandparents have a favorite uncle or aunt?
_____
_____
_____
_____

Was anyone named after their grand parents, or aunt or uncle? Who named the children? Were they named after a famous person or president?
_____
_____
_____
_____

Do you know if their last name was changed from the slave master's last name to something different? For example; name was changed to Freeman from slavemaster's name? Was a letter dropped or added to differentiate from a specific culture to Americanize the name?

_____
_____
_____
_____

Are there any stories that have been passed down about certain family members? For example; Old Uncle Ned killed a man and had to be sent to a family member's home in another state or town far away!

_____
_____
_____
_____

Does the story about uncle Ned have any validity? Did he marry and have kids? Are there any newspaper articles about this? Are there any death certificates proving the person was killed or stating how the person was killed or died?

_____
_____
_____
_____

Did you lose track of any family members who moved to another city or state? Example; Uncle Ned moved to Kansas and no one knows much more about him.

_____
_____
_____
_____

Part Four:
Quotes

"We are our ancestors' wildest dreams."

– Unknown

"Our history is our strength. Our culture is our power. Our unity is our future.

— Unknown

"A PEOPLE WITHOUT THE KNOWLEDGE OF THEIR PAST HISTORY, ORIGIN, AND CULTURE IS LIKE A TREE WITHOUT ROOTS."

– MARCUS GARVEY

"History has shown us that courage can be contagious, and hope can take on a life of its own."

– Michelle Obama

"To accept one's past—one's history—is not the same as drowning in it; it is learning how to use it."

– James Baldwin

"We were never meant to survive, yet here we stand. Strong. Proud. Unbreakable."

- Audre Lorde

"I AM MY ANCESTORS' STRENGTH, MY FAMILY'S RESILIENCE, AND MY OWN GREATEST HOPE."

– UNKNOWN

"Preserve your history, for in it lies the power of your ancestors and the wisdom for your future."

– Nnamdi Azikiwe

"You may not control all the events that happen to you, but you can decide not to be reduced by them."

– Maya Angelou

"We have to tell our own story, because if we don't, someone else will, and they will not tell it right."

– Chinua Achebe

"The most common way people give up their power is by thinking they don't have any."

— Alice Walker

"Hold fast to dreams, for if dreams die, life is a broken-winged bird that cannot fly."

– Langston Hughes

"Culture is not a luxury, it is a necessity. Without it, we are lost."

— Amílcar Cabral

"If you know whence you came, there is really no limit to where you can go."

– James Baldwin

"A RACE THAT IS SOLELY DEPENDENT UPON ANOTHER FOR ITS ECONOMIC EXISTENCE SOONER OR LATER DIES."

– CARTER G. WOODSON

"The Black skin is not a badge of shame, but rather a glorious symbol of national greatness."

Marcus Garvey

"We did not come this far only to come this far. Our ancestors paved the way, and now it is our turn to build."

– Unknown

"An individual has not started living until he can rise above the narrow confines of his individualistic concerns to the broader concerns of all humanity."

– Martin Luther King Jr.

"We must unlearn the lies
we have been taught and
relearn the truth about
who we are."

— Malidoma Patrice Somé

"Liberate the minds of men and ultimately you will liberate the bodies of men."

– Marcus Garvey

"To be Black and conscious in America is to be in a constant state of rage."

— James Baldwin

"The function of freedom is to free someone else."

— Toni Morrison

"It is not taboo to go back and fetch what you forgot."

– Akan Proverb (Sankofa)

"Your silence will not protect you."

– Audre Lorde

"True leadership strengthens others and builds a legacy that outlives the leader."

Nelson Mandela

"A UNITED PEOPLE, STRIVING TO ACHIEVE A GREAT FEAT, WILL ALWAYS EMERGE VICTORIOUS."

– NELSON MANDELA

"We are Africans not because we were born in Africa, but because Africa was born in us."

– Kwame Nkrumah

"Your story is what you have, what you will always have. It is something to own."

– Michelle Obama

"When we stand tall in our truth, we honor the ones who came before us and pave the way for those yet to come."

– Unknown

"There is no greater agony than bearing an untold story inside you."

Maya Angelou

"Change will not come if we wait for some other person or some other time. We are the ones we've been waiting for. We are the change that we seek."

— Barack Obama

Part Five:
Additional Resources

Websites

1. African American Genealogy (National Archives)
https://www.archives.gov/research/african-americans
   - Provides a wealth of resources and guides for African American genealogy research, including records related to slavery, military service, and more.

2. Afro-American Historical and Genealogical Society, Inc.
https://www.aahgs.org/
   -a non-profit 501(c)3, which strives to preserve African-ancestored family history, genealogy, and cultural diversity by teaching research techniques and disseminating information throughout the community.

3. FamilySearch African American Resources
https://www.familysearch.org/en/united-states/
   - Offers a vast collection of African American historical records, including census data, Freedmen's Bureau records, and other valuable resources for tracing African ancestry.

4. Smithsonian National Museum of African American History and Culture
https://www.si.edu/museums/african-american-museum
   - Provides resources for family history research, including guides and links to archival collections, oral histories, and other records.

5. Ancestry.com's African American Collection
www.ancestry.com/c/african-american
- A subscription-based service

6. National Genealogical Society
National Genealogical Society or local chapters

- Is here to help individuals learn about their family history. They are a non-profit organization headquartered in Falls Church, Virginia. For 120 years, they have been the leader in teaching genealogical research skills and providing a pathway to scholarly work.

Books

1. **"The Warmth of Other Suns: The Epic Story of America's Great Migration" by Isabel Wilkerson**
   - Chronicles the migration of African Americans from the rural South to urban centers in the North and West, offering deep insights into the legacy of this movement.

2. **"Finding Your Roots: The Official Companion to the PBS Series" by Henry Louis Gates Jr.**
   - A guide to exploring family history, including African American genealogy, with practical advice and case studies from the PBS series.

3. **"Black Roots: A Beginner's Guide to Tracing the African American Family Tree" by Tony Burroughs**
   - Provides detailed steps and strategies for tracing African American genealogy, from finding records to understanding historical contexts.

4. **"In Search of Our Roots: How 19 Extraordinary African Americans Reclaimed Their Past" by Henry Louis Gates Jr.**
   - A companion to the PBS series, this book shares the genealogical journeys of prominent African Americans, offering inspiration and guidance for others.

5. **"The Slave Trade: The Story of the Atlantic Slave Trade: 1440-1870" by Hugh Thomas**
   - A comprehensive history of the transatlantic slave trade, providing crucial context for understanding African American ancestry and history.

Part Six:
Meet the Author

Meet The Author

Laurene, a Texas native, has a deep love for African American history and preserving cultural legacies. Recently retired from the telecommunications industry, she now dedicates her time to researching and uncovering her family's rich history. During the 2020 pandemic, Laurene rediscovered family treasures, including letters and artifacts, that shed light on her ancestors' lives.

She grew up in the home her grandparents built in Mt. Haven, an East Texas Freedom Colony outside Jacksonville, Texas. Laurene has always cherished stories from "the old days," particularly those from her elders. Her passion for history and culture drives her to inspire others to honor their past, celebrate their identity, and preserve their legacy for future generations.

Please scan this QR code to visit our site and book Laurene for your next event. www.ourpastourway.com

Made in the USA
Coppell, TX
21 April 2025

48509017R00056